THE YEARLING

CHARLES A. RAINES
DEPARTMENT OF ENGLISH
CITY UNIVERSITY OF NEW YORK

MONARCH
PRESS

Published by
MONARCH PRESS
a Simon & Schuster division of
Gulf & Western Corporation
Simon & Schuster Building
1230 Avenue of the Americas
New York, N.Y. 10020

Standard Book Number: 0-671-00859-5

Library of Congress Catalog Card Number: 66-27317

MONARCH PRESS and colophon are trademarks
of Simon & Schuster, registered in the U.S. Patent
and Trademark Office.

Printed in the United States of America

CONTENTS

INTRODUCTION

BIOGRAPHY: Marjorie Kinnan Rawlings was born in Washington, D.C., in 1896 and died in Florida in 1953. After graduating from the University of Wisconsin in 1918 she became a newspaper reporter. She worked for the Louisville, Kentucky, *Courier-Journal* and for the Rochester, New York, *Journal.* She also worked from time to time in advertising and publicity. In 1928 she went to live in Cross Creek, Florida, where she owned an orange grove. She became acquainted with the Florida hammock country and its people, and in 1930 submitted to *Scribner's Magazine* some sketches of the country and its people. In 1931 some of these were published in *Scribner's Magazine* under the title "Cracker Childings." Later she published stories, all having to do with the Florida Crackers, in *Scribner's, Harper's, The Saturday Evening Post, The New Yorker* and elsewhere. In 1931 she lived for several weeks in the Florida scrub country, observing the ways of the people living there. As a result she wrote *South Moon Under,* which was published in 1933. This book dealt with the "shiners" (or persons who made their living primarily from moonshining), much like the Forresters of *The Yearling.* This book was a selection of the Book-of-the Month Club and was well received by the critics. After the publication of this book she went to England to gather material for another novel. In the meantime, at the suggestion of her editor, she became interested in writing a book for children. As a result of this interest she wrote *The Yearling,* which was published in 1938. This book was selected as the Pulitzer Prize Novel for that year. Although she wrote other books, her only other popularly successful work was *Cross Creek,* published in 1942. This was a collection of essays, character sketches, narratives and short stories, dealing with her Florida scrub country environment.

LOCAL COLOR AND REALISM: As a reporter it was natural that Mrs. Rawlings should have written primarily from observation. In this sense her work falls in with a great deal of the "local color" writing of her time. This was primarily reportage of a given area of the country. A number of these writers became popular for their exposition of a particular locality and its customs. Mark Twain had aroused interest in the customs of the Mississippi river folk about the time of the Civil War and in the later part of the century. Bret Harte and others chronicled the people of the Southwest and West. Later Willa Cather wrote about the Midwest and Southwest. There was much interest in isolated localities and the people living in them. While some of this writing was not merely reportage, much of it was. Mrs. Rawlings herself pointed out in a letter to her editor that she had kept notes on the Florida Crackers and observed them closely, as though she were writing a documentary. In a sense *The Yearling* is a piece of reportage on these people and the effort is to record them exactly as they lived. She reports the wildlife and vegetation of the region in minute detail. The reader of *The Yearling* becomes intimately acquainted not only with the people of this region and their customs and way of life, but with the physical and natural surroundings. In the manner of a reporter, Mrs. Rawlings remains objective and detached. She makes no real judgment of these people, but merely reports the facts as she sees them. In this sense the book is realistic in its detail and in its treatment of the life of the region. The facts of the book came from actual observation by Mrs. Rawlings. She went on bear hunts and fishing trips, lived in the deep scrub country and talked with people who knew the life of this region intimately. Her fidelity to the facts was so accurate that some newspapers in Florida became alarmed when the book was published, claiming it gave a distorted picture of the state. But Mrs. Rawlings could stand on her work because she could substantiate the accuracy of its details. As Mark Twain did in *Huckleberry Finn,* Mrs. Rawlings simply superimposed a fictional story on a mass of accurate detail.

SOME LITERARY PARALLELS: The reader of *The Yearling* will compare it to other similar books. When she wrote this novel her editor, Maxwell Perkins, had suggested she write a book like *Huckleberry Finn,* or other children's books. The comparison between these books is obvious. They are both about young boys growing up in the wilderness. But the comparison ends there since Huck's world is very different from Jody's. There are other books that deal with youth growing into maturity in a frontier situation posing problems of survival. Rolvaag's *Giants in the Earth,* Willa Cather's *My Antonia,* John Steinbeck's *The Red Pony and* William Faulkner's *The Bear* all come to mind. Probably what distinguishes *The Yearling* is the attitude of its characters. Mrs. Rawlings wrote that she was "astonished by the utter lack of bleakness or despair" on the part of these people. This was a characteristic of the pioneer people recorded by Steinbeck and others, but it has probably nowhere been more emphasized than in this book.

THE STYLE: The most outstanding attribute of Mrs. Rawlings' style throughout *The Yearling* is her lack of intervention as the writer. Mrs. Rawlings uses symbolism sparingly but effectively. The yearling itself is a symbol of helplessness and innocence and then of wildness. The sinkhole is a symbolic resting place for Jody. She does not introduce philosophical or psychological motivations into the story. There is no attempt to explain why the people act as they do. Mrs. Rawlings merely reports what she has observed without giving an explanation for it. Although most of the characters in the book have developed a philosophy of life, it is stated very simply and without elaboration. Mrs. Rawlings adds no interpretation to this nor does she judge it. This is partially substantiated by the third person point of view from which the story is told. Any judgment of the characters or implications drawn about their point of view toward life merely implied. It is left for the reader to supply his own interpretation to the story and to explain the actions of the characters. The dialects used by the people are always accurate and add to the authenticity of the book. Mrs. Rawlings has recorded these speech patterns with a sharp ear both for pronunciations and for expressions used among the Florida hammock-country people. The simplicity of her writing style is thus reflected in the simplicity of the speech of the characters as well as their simple way of life.

ANALYSIS OF *THE YEARLING*

CHAPTERS 1–4

As the book opens it is a balmy Friday afternoon in April. Jody Baxter has left the cabin in which he lives with his mother and father in the hammock country of Florida to hoe in the corn field. He is diverted by the beauty of the spring day and feels more like playing than working. He decides to follow the bees to the spring and see if there is a bee-tree there. He justifies this action on the grounds that gathering honey would be more important than hoeing the corn. When he arrives at the spring he decides to make a flutter-mill, like the one his friend Oliver Hutto made for him. This he does, and sits watching it turn over in the water. Soon he falls asleep in a fine mist of rain. When he wakes up he returns to the cabin to find that his father is doing his chores for him. His mother has not missed him and his father is not angry. The next day it is discovered that a huge bear, named Slewfoot (because he has lost a toe in a bear trap) has killed the Baxters' sow. Jody's father agrees to let Jody accompany him on a hunt for the bear. They set out with their three dogs and the father's primitive muzzle-loading gun and finally bring Slewfoot to bay at the creek. Jody's father tries to shoot the bear, but his gun backfires. Old Julia, the hound, is badly wounded by Slewfoot and the bear gets away.

COMMENT: Man and Nature. What strikes the reader most in the beginning of this book is the placidity of the scene and the emphasis placed on the natural environment. When we first meet Jody he seems to be blended into the natural scene, which Mrs. Rawlings describes in great detail. He appears to be one with nature. There hardly seems to be a separation between his own feelings as a person and the general feeling emanating from his natural surroundings. It is spring, a time when nature is at its height. The flowers are blooming, the bees are buzzing about, and there is a proliferation of natural growth. Even the air itself is surfeited with this feeling. The spring fever that Jody experiences symbolizes the placidity of the natural surrounding. April is indeed a traditional time of happiness and placidity. It is a time of youth.

Jody does not question this environment of which he is a part. Rather, his strongest feeling is that he is in fact a part of it in a mystical way. He feels he is connected with the creek, which flows to the lake; the lake in turn is a part of the river, which flows to the sea. Just as April is a time of youth, it is also a time of change. Like youth it looks forward to changes to be brought about as the seasons progress. In this way it is ominous. Like nature itself, Jody will change. He will go through a cycle, like the seasons of the year which he passes through during the course of this book. He is at a time in his life, at the age of thirteen, when he will change significantly. Mrs. Rawlings is interested in this change as a passage from childhood to manhood. Thus the opening scene, in which we find a traditional placidity and happiness and the pervasiveness of nature, serves not only to introduce us to Jody and his surroundings, but to the omnipresence of change. Further, the mill-wheel itself stands as a symbol of mutability, or change. This is Jody's attempt to arrest nature and to create something permanent.

At this point Jody is highly conversant with his natural surrounding. One reviewer pointed out that Jody is a sort of St. Francis, in the sense that he seems to have a sort of natural, almost religious, affinity with animals and other natural beings. Concerning nature, there are only two qualifications that Jody makes in his own mind: (1) He separates the animate from the inanimate; (2) He separates the practical from the impractical. Although he would like to have a pet of his own, he finds that the dogs, which might ordinarily have a function as pets, have a purely practical function. The same is true of Trixie, the cow, and the pigs. They are there only for the purpose of providing milk and meat. Jody therefore searches for something "impractical" to which he can attach himself. He searches for relief from the overburdening practicality of his own life.

In this first section he learns another separation in nature: some natural objects are a menace and must be removed. When Slewfoot comes to the corral and kills the sow, Jody becomes suddenly aware of a law of nature: both man and beast must provide themselves with food or starve to death. Slewfoot is, in effect, by killing the sow, doing the same thing man must do. He must kill for his food, or die. This is yet another practicality with which Jody is faced and, once he realizes this, his appetite for something impractical—a pet which will serve not only as a companion but as a symbol of that area in which it is not necessary to be practical—is intensified. When Jody goes to the spring instead of hoeing the corn, this dramatically displays Jody's dilemma. Although this action may appear from an adult point of view to be incidental, it must be borne in mind that to a child nothing is ever really incidental. His father justifies Jody's action on the grounds that Jody will not always be a child, and that once he is an adult he will discover that he is overcome with the necessities of living. Penny Baxter, Jody's father, draws this inference from his own childhood, which had been severe and restrictive, not only because his father, a minister, had very puritanical ideas, but because the business of obtain-

ing food and staying alive had been particularly difficult. Penny recognizes the necessity of allowing as
much freedom to Jody as is possible. We will see how
this dilemma works out in the end.

Jody's Relationship to His Parents.　From the beginning it is evident that Jody's relationship to his father
is different from his relationship to his mother. The
fact that his mother is more strict is shown by his fear
that she will be angry with him when she finds he has
not done the hoeing. On the other hand, his father
takes the attitude that any boy would want to play on
a beautiful spring day such as this one. Yet Ora
Baxter, his mother, does not take this particular in-
fraction too seriously. Nothing has been seriously
damaged by Jody's action. However, this looks forward to later actions which Jody's mother considers
far more serious and plants a justification for her later
actions. Penny Baxter, as has been noted, is more
likely to interpret Jody in terms of his own boyhood,
and, like many fathers, hopes Jody will not have as
hard a life as he has had. This is also heightened by
Penny's inclination to gentleness and honesty. Penny
points out to Jody that the men must stick together. In
a sense Jody and his father live in a different world
together—their duties and goals are different. They
are both men and it is up to Penny to teach Jody the
ways of women. They are naturally drawn together.

The attention given Jody by both parents, and the
willingness on the part of both of them to take an
understanding attitude toward Jody, is intensified by
the fact that he is the only surviving child of many
they have had. He is not simply an only child, but an
only *surviving* child. Jody is himself a comfort against
the grief of their loss. It should be observed that Jody
is totally dependent on his mother and father for

support—for his food, bed and clothing. His obedience partially grows out of this. Unlike Huckleberry Finn he cannot depend upon his own ingenuity to support himself. As yet he does not even own a gun that would enable him to support himself if he wished. In fact, what is emphasized in this opening section of the book is Jody's warm relationship with his parents. Under the circumstances they are an almost ideal family. Jody has no real fear of his parents and feels very close to his father. This is in contrast, it might be noted, to characters like Huckleberry Finn, whose father treated him cruelly and abandoned him. On the other hand, *The Yearling* is itself the story of the closeness of a familial relationship. Jody's only problem comes as one of understanding when he mistakes a necessity of living as a betrayal.

The Theme of Isolation. The various forms of isolation introduced in this first section of the book serve the basic purpose of showing the characters in a more intense state of survival than if they were placed in a social situation where dependence on others would be possible. The first indication of isolation is Jody's own desire to get away from the cabin to the spring, "a secret and lovely place." Here he can live in his own private world, even disconnected from his parents. This is a peaceful place where he can develop his fantasies without the interference of reality, except that which he produces for himself.

But the essence of any isolation is that it ironically points up the necessity of dependence on others. No sooner has Jody isolated himself than he wishes for a connection with something. It is true that his isolation intensifies his feeling of a mystical connection with nature, but this is offset by his return to the cabin, his eagerness for food, and the warmth he feels when he lies down to sleep beside his father. The secretiveness of this place at the spring is a manifestation of his inner self. What he finds here as a desirable state of feeling he does not yet recognize as aloneness. In other words, isolation here serves him well as long as he is conscious of the fact that he will be able to return to a world in which he will be received as a part of something else. The feeling of secretiveness is also different from the longing for possession. Like most children, he has a desire to repeat the pattern of which he is a part. He is possessed by his parents, and commanded by them. He also would like to act out this adult role by possessing and commanding something of his own. His longing is something like that in a girl's longing for a doll. Through the doll the girl can repeat the pattern of which she is a part and look forward to an adult role to be taken on in reality. Thus Jody's isolation at the spring represents a sort of dream-state in which he acts out a reality to come. Jody is, as a child, isolated from the adult world which he has not yet been allowed to enter. In fact, the hunt for the bear is his first significant entry into this adult world. Jody's creation of the flutter-mill, for example, is not an incidental act, but is representative of his desire to create and control in the manner of his father and mother.

Another aspect of isolation lies in one of the basic effects of this study of Jody: the contrast between the life of nature and the life of society. Mrs. Rawlings is apparently most interested in discovering man's natural inclinations as opposed to his social inclinations. By showing a family that is for the most part cut off from society, she is better able to study these natural inclinations. For this reason it may be assumed that it is more than circumstantial that the family lives apart on an "island." It is indeed significant that this is not really an island in the common sense of the word, but an island of pines in an area otherwise thickly grown over with scrub. The physical "island" then is symbolic of the physical and spiritual isolation of the family. But perhaps the most significant point to be made is that Penny Baxter *chose* to isolate himself from society. He considered the company of wild animals less dangerous than the company of people. Also he had been the victim of numerous psychic wounds. He had been in the war and had been subjected to various unpleasant relationships. His observation about humans is that they are more often bickering than not. In this attitude he reflects what may be recognized as the typical American frontiersman's point of view of rugged individualism.

Jody's search for isolation thus recapitulates that of his father. This is later corroborated by the Baxter's relationship with the Forresters and the Forresters with the Huttos. While Mrs. Rawlings does not elaborate upon this flight from society or make it the center of attention as, for example, Mark Twain did in *Huckleberry Finn,* it is at least implicit in her work that the Baxters share the feeling of the Romantics that it is better to be one with nature than to be one with other people. This isolation, it may be noted, is made possible by the fact that at the time of the action of this book it was still possible to live off the land and from the provisions of game and wild growth. In more recent times this possibility has been considerably diminished, and one of the charms of this book is that it provides a picture of life in the United States before the movement toward urbanization.

The Theme of Initiation. The narration of the bear hunt in this first section introduces the theme of initiation. It may first be noted that Jody lives in what

anthropologists and sociologists refer to as a traditional society. This means that the children are
brought up to repeat the pattern set for them by their
parents. In order for the parents to insure the recapitu-
lation of this pattern, the child must be "initiated,"
that is, he is shown the way of life, in gradual stages,
and he is expected to follow. It is assumed on the part
of the parents that the structure of the society in which
the child grows up to manhood will remain essentially
the same. In fact there is a concerted effort by the
adults to see to it that this pattern is maintained
without severe changes. Thus the initiation is carried
on in the form of indoctrination. The bear hunt itself
serves as an indoctrination for the child Jody. The
father assumes that Jody will need this information as
he grows up. Thus he learns certain aspects of the
ritual of the bear hunt. He is instructed, in other
words, in a pattern which will lead to his manhood.
Underlying this instruction by his father is the idea
that Jody, as a man, will be obliged to learn the crafty
ways of wild animals in order to be able to overcome
them.

The instruction that Jody receives at the hands of his
father also carries with it the lesson that there is
cruelty involved. When the dogs attack Slewfoot, for
example, Jody is horrified, and he is repulsed by the
bloodshed and violence. When his father asks him how
he liked the bear hunt, Jody replies that he enjoyed the
chase, but was frightened by the violence. Jody also
learns the courage and bravery of the dogs, Julia and
Rip, and the uselessness of the feist (little dog). These,
together with the father, stand as examples for Jody in
his own personal life.

Some other elements of traditional initiation enter into
this. There is the ordeal of the hunt, which Jody learns

more about later. That is, the idea that the adult male must sacrifice himself to privation and hardship in order to protect and provide. There is the intensification of the idea of the community of the males. After having been on the hunt with his father, Jody feels closer to him than ever. He feels secure in the knowledge that his father will protect him and that he will eventually, as a result of his instruction, be able to protect and provide for himself. At this point the father dominates and handles the gun. He has the superior knowledge and experience and serves as the instructor. The bear itself serves as a sort of demigod and there is a code, almost of a religious nature, to be followed. Jody, as the child being initiated, must learn this code. First he learns to respect the bear, an enormous and wily creature, more mysterious and cunning than the other wild animals and capable of greater destruction and greater wrath than the others. Then his father points out that the bear is being killed for a purpose, not merely for sport. While the Forresters will kill a bear whether they need the meat or not, Penny, who is more religious and more traditional, will not kill for meat when he does not need it. This is a basic law entailing respect for wild animals and appreciation for their position as a part of nature. There is an unwritten code of ethics to be followed, based primarily on what Penny refers to as honesty.

CHAPTERS 5–7

Penny decides to take the feist to the Forresters, who live a few miles away at Forrester's Island, and attempt to trade him for a new gun. When they arrive at the Forresters' cabin there is a noisy and boisterous greeting. Penny and Jody accept the Forresters' invitation to stay for the noon meal. Afterward, Penny tells the story of the bear hunt, in the meantime arousing Lem Forrester's interest in the feist.

Finally Lem trades a new English gun to Penny in exchange for the feist. He does this on condition that Penny allow him to be in on the shooting of Slewfoot if the opportunity presents itself. Penny and Fodder-wing, a crippled child of the Forresters' who has gotten his name from his attempt to fly by jumping off a barn using fodder as "wings," play together with Fodder-wing's pets. Penny agrees to let Jody spend the night with the Forresters. Before dawn the next morning a fox enters the house being chased by the dogs and the entire group wakes up. The Forresters begin to drink corn liquor and dance to music played on a fiddle. After breakfast Buck Forrester rides Jody home on his horse.

COMMENT: A Contrast. One of the chief functions of this section of the book is to contrast the two families: the Baxters and the Forresters. This contrast serves not only to bring out certain characteristics of Jody and his family, but to further the themes introduced in the first section. In the first place, it is obvious that the Baxters are a staid, devoted family bent on honesty and goodness in the sense that they live only within the limitations of their immediate needs. Everything they do is directed toward survival without treading on the freedom of others. While the Forresters themselves are not intrinsically evil people, they are a more socializing group than the Baxters.

The fact that they make their living primarily from trading and from selling illegal liquor made in a still that they maintain, and that they will kill for food even when it is not necessary, points up their indifference to the code by which the Baxters live. The Baxters do not begrudge the relative opulence in which the Forresters live because of the fact that the Forresters have gone outside the limits of the code in order to obtain this opulence. As long as it has been obtained dishonestly, it cannot be an object of envy. There is also the matter of respectability. This perhaps springs from the background of the Baxters. Penny is the son of a minister and Ma Baxter has come from one of the respectable families of the town. Part of Ma Baxter's and Penny's disapproval of the Forresters grows out of this puritanical respectability. Thus Ma Baxter would disapprove of Jody's playing mumbletypeg on the floor as he does with Fodder-wing at the Forresters' house, and of the frolicsome nature of the Forrester family.

It is therefore a peculiarity of the Baxters that while they live in isolation and are not particularly solicitous of the approval of others, they nevertheless attempt to maintain this respectability. This can only be said to spring from their puritanical background, which has instilled in them cleanliness and frugality as virtues. Hard work, patience and fortitude are intrinsic in the Baxters, not as virtues that they have created for themselves, but as virtues that have been handed down to them and which serve as the best means toward insuring the survival of their code. The Forresters represent both an intrusion upon this code and the possibility for unhappiness when it is broken.

Penny's attitude that people usually bicker among themselves is pointed out by example in the Forresters, and this idea is developed later in the book. The quarrel that breaks out over which dog has wet the floor is an example, albeit mostly good natured, of this point. But Mrs. Rawlings carries this contrast further to show the difference in necessities put upon the Baxters and the Forresters. While there are six Forrester sons (Buck, Mill-Wheel, Gabby, Pack, Arch and Lem) to carry on the necessary work of the Forrester family, Penny has been denied this particular opulence by fate because all his children have died except Jody. Since there are more Forresters to do the work and to hunt, they have a somewhat easier time of it. Also there is the difference in stature of the two families. Penny is a small man and, although he is tough enough for his size, he simply is not capable of the same amount of work as the huge Forrester boys with all their strength and endurance. This helps make the point, too, that Penny's struggle for survival is even more heroic and commendable since he is working against these odds. Thus when Penny is ill or otherwise unable to work, he has only Jody to rely on.

Another reason why Mrs. Rawlings develops this contrast between the two families is to show the various levels of society in this geographical area. The Forresters represent the wild frontier type that is likely to be found in many local-color stories of the South and Southwest. This has in fact been a long tradition in American literature. For example, anyone who has read *Huckleberry Finn* will remember that Mark Twain introduced a number of these types, such as Miss Watson and the Widow Douglass, staid puritanical types, and the King and the Duke, who are wild and amoral types, and many others.

This type of free-swinging, individualistic and often brawling frontiersman has often been used not only for interest in the characters themselves, but for comic effect. The original quarrel over the dog in Chapter 5, the incident of the varmint running through the house, and the music, dance and drinking in the early morning hours all add a note of levity to the story. This is one reason why Jody so enjoys visiting the Forresters. He expects this kind of frivolity and light-heartedness and gets much pleasure from it. This is not to say that the Baxters themselves are not on occasion witty and given to lightness, but their outlook on life is more serious and intent. This grows out of a certain native intelligence on the part of the Baxters, which is displayed when Penny successfully convinces Lem Forrester of the value of the feist, which is really worthless, and trades the feist for a new English gun. While neither of these families is very highly educated, although Jody has received some instruction from a teacher, the Baxters are natively more intelligent, perceptive and morally sensitive. As was pointed out in the discussion of the first section of the book, this occurs because the Baxters have a stronger feeling of their oneness with nature and a more sensitive moral sense of the rights of others, and even of the animals.

Jody and Fodder-wing. Another important function of this section of the book is to show the relationship between Jody and Fodder-wing. First it should be noted that Jody again displays his native sense of goodness and gentleness in not "pestering" the crippled Fodder-wing as some other people do. Further, Jody is attracted to Fodder-wing because of the fact that Fodder-wing is allowed to have pets. This is considered an extravagance by Jody's parents because pets would eat up a good deal of the food so difficult for them to obtain. Naturally Jody derives a great deal of pleasure from playing with these pets.

But the connection goes farther than this in that Fodder-wing represents to Jody the presence of the impracticality spoken of in the discussion of the first section. Since Fodder-wing had been born a cripple and had injured himself even more when he jumped from a barn in an attempt to fly using fodder as wings, he is not called upon to participate in the work or to contribute to the necessities of living. To Jody he represents that area in which practicality is not necessary. Fodder-wing is not expected either to develop a moral sense as Jody is because Fodder-wing is slow-witted. In spite of these handicaps Fodder-wing stands to Jody for a natural simplicity, which attracts him.

Jody learns from this crippled, slow-witted character the true meaning of gentleness, kindness and regard for others. What Mrs. Rawlings seems to concentrate on is the native human instinct. In this character she can emphasize even further the idea that true virtue has little to do with intelligence or physical ability. It is something, rather, which is given in nature. Fodder-wing has an intense personal understanding of the animals who are his pets and they of him. Jody recognizes this as a gift Fodder-wing has, although he may have been deprived of other gifts.

In addition to his native gentleness, Fodder-wing also possesses imagination, something that is not allowed in the world of practicality in which the others live. His visions of the Spaniards who passed through Florida in early times fires Jody's imagination, even though others look upon these visions merely as a manifestation of Fodder-wing's lack of sense. Although it may only be momentary, Fodder-wing's presence allows Jody to pass into this world of instinct and imagination. He is allowed to participate in Fodder-wing's attempts to get free of his burdens. This is why Fodder-wing appears as a lovable rather than a grotesque character in the book.

Legend and Fact.   The two legends discussed in this section of the book show imagination on the one hand and reality on the other. Significantly, Jody is exposed to both. The legend of the Spaniards is introduced when Jody and his father are riding through the woods on the way to Forrester's Island. Jody notices some blazes, or axe marks, on some very old trees and inquires how they got there. (Mrs. Rawlings, by the way, does not explain why Jody has not noticed these blazes before, even though he has no doubt passed this way many times.) This is a legend from the past and has survived only as a vestige of the past. Penny's lack of interest in this legend shows that he feels it doesn't have very much to do with the present. But Jody is interested in it, not only out of childish curiosity, but, as has been pointed out, as a manifestation of the imagination.

Later, when Fodder-wing speaks of the Spaniards and claims to have seen them, Jody's curiosity is further aroused. This allows him a momentary flight of fantasy, but the real business at hand has to do with the legend at hand: the hunt for Slewfoot. This is something that Jody himself has participated in as a myth-in-the-making. Jody later remarks that he will be able to pass this story on to his children. The adults, Penny and the Forresters, are interested in this because it has an immediate application. The bear is still at large and must be hunted and killed. The adults are much more interested in this story than in the story of the Spaniards, because the bear story is more realistic in its detail. Also, when Ma Baxter had expressed disapproval of Jody's visiting the wild Forresters, Penny had defended his visit on the grounds that Jody needed experience in the company of men.

Thus the story of the bear hunt and the other hunting stories told at the Forrester cabin serve as a part of Jody's instruction by the adults. The tales and legends themselves, it may be noted, are a part of the socialization of the persons involved. In this sense the recounting of tales serves as a means of introducing the young to relationships with others. The talk among the men, with the women left out, also is a part of the initiation which Jody undergoes. During this process he has a chance to separate truth from falsehood and the practical from the impractical.

In addition to this, Jody is exposed to models of heroism, sacrifice and endurance. Jody's concern about Penny's passing off the feist as a useful dog although he is in fact worthless bears this out. Penny points out that he has not in fact distorted the truth. He has truthfully informed Lem as to the feist's sorry performance during the bear hunt, but Penny's reliance on the psychological effect of his presentation of the feist wins out. Thus Jody sees an example of adult relationships in which there is no violation of the truth, but a healthy distortion of it. Penny has successfully used Fodder-wing's imaginative effect to gain his ends. This is a lesson which comes back to Jody at a later point in the book.

Foreshadowing and Subplot. It may be noted that one of Mrs. Rawlings' most often used devices in the structure of this book is that of foreshadowing. This is the method of planting in advance something that hints at an action to take place later in the story. This serves not only to heighten the suspense, but to lay a logical groundwork for the occurrence of this action. An example of this occurs at the end of Chapter 7 when Lem mentions Twink Weatherby. Jody remarks that it is understood that she is Oliver Hutto's girl. Lem's immediate reaction of anger shows something about this moody, explosive character developed at greater length later, and plants the basis for the feud between Lem and Oliver. This also introduces a subplot; that is, a story line parallel to the major story.

In this book the story mainly has to do with Jody and the fawn, but underneath this is the story of the

Forresters and the Huttos. As an underlying plot, this helps to move the story by showing certain contrasts and ironic events. Principally Jody's basic gentleness and gentility is contrasted with Lem's hot-tempered nature and Jody's position as a child is contrasted with the position he will have to assume as an adult, especially in relation to girls.

CHAPTERS 8–12

Jody returns home from the Forresters' to find that Penny has killed a deer. Jody goes to the sinkhole for water and ruminates on the mysteries of nature. Penny joins him at the sinkhole and they talk together. The next morning Jody is ill as a result of eating too many brierberries, although he does not tell his mother this. After Jody recovers, he and Penny go fishing. The next day Jody and Penny set out to hunt for deer, which they plan to take to Volusia to trade for supplies. While hunting they come upon two bear cubs in a tree. Jody wants to take one of them for a pet, but Penny says they are too large. Jody has the thrill of shooting his first deer. Penny dresses the deer and they proceed to Volusia. They first go to Boyles' store. From the store they go to Grandma Hutto's house. At daylight the next morning, Oliver Hutto, Grandma Hutto's son who is a sailor, arrives from a trip to the tropics. He tells stories of his sailing adventures and brings gifts for all. After they have eaten, Oliver leaves to take a gift to his girl friend, Twink Weatherby. Oliver gets into a fight with the Forrester boys as a result of his attention to Twink. Penny jumps into the fight to defend Oliver. Jody tries to fight Lem, but is knocked out.

COMMENT: The Hunger Motif. The primary function of Chapter 8 is to emphasize a motif, or recurrent theme, of the novel. Some attitudes toward survival have already been pointed out. Up to this point it is clear that the major concern of the Baxters is survival. But they take a particular point of view toward this. They are very economical in their consumption of available food and avoid any indulgence for its own sake. Whereas the Forresters are apt to surround themselves with what the Baxters would regard as luxuries, the Baxters are inclined to take only game that they need. The lives of the Baxters are essentially centered about this minimum level of survival and their attitudes and activities are for the most part formed about this. Most of what they do is of a practical nature directed toward survival.

But Penny is constantly aware of the possibility of falling below a minimum level of survival. One of his intentions as Jody's teacher is to make him aware of the necessity of maintaining at least a minimum level of survival and of the possibility of the loss of this level. Up to this point Jody is prevented from keeping a pet because it might endanger the food supply. Thus when Jody returns home from visiting the Forresters he is at first disappointed that Penny has killed a deer in his absence. Penny, however, points out that the pleasures of hunting are less important than the provision of food. Jody's disappointment at missing the hunt is abated when he realizes the deer will provide a good meal. Also important is the fact that Jody's repulsion at the dead carcass of the deer is overcome when he makes this distinction. Thus Jody must adjust himself to accepting the destruction of nature for the practical purpose of survival. This is a necessary adjustment in the primitive type of society in which Jody lives. Ironically he learns to love nature and become one with it, yet he must live from its provisions, just as the other animals do. Jody does not revolt against this destruction of nature when he realizes the principle of necessity involved. Once he sits down to eat the deer that has been shot, he realizes the justification of the killing.

At this point in the book, the emphasis on Jody's pleasure at such provision and his enjoyment of abundance foreshadows the period when the rain storm comes and food is in short supply. It should be pointed out once again that the Baxters also make a virtue of their attitude toward minimum survival provision. Thus Ma Baxter deprecates the frivolity of the Forresters on the grounds that it has no practical application. Jody's struggle between practicality and impracticality comes into play here. Unlike his mother, he does not find fault with the Forresters' frivolity. He has not yet learned to subdue his impractical passions.

The Microcosm. The discussion of the sinkhole where Jody goes to get water serves two purposes: it furthers the hunger motif in that it shows a different kind of necessary provision and it furthers the idea of Jody's closeness to nature. The fact that the Baxters have had for twenty years to retrieve water from the sinkhole not only points up one of their hardships, but shows their capacity for endurance and survival. Jody's ruminations while at the sinkhole return the reader to the opening scene at the creek. Again we see Jody in a mood of introversion, pointing up the sensitivity of his nature. Jody thinks about his aloneness as a human being, but is comforted by his ability to make of this natural scene a private world of his own in which he can enjoy a private relationship with the animals and with the natural surrounding. His very aloneness and isolation builds up in him a spiritual power he would not otherwise have. He relates himself to this world and makes it his own. It becomes a microcosm in the sense not only that it is the only world he knows, unlike Oliver Hutto who has traveled widely, but in that he has made it his own. His familiarity with this world of pine trees, the cabin, the animals he sees, and the activities he undergoes here gives him a sense of belonging and identity. His tendency is to interpret life in terms of this microcosm in which he lives. His desire for a pet, which he expresses at this point, thus is a desire to become more deeply identified with this microcosm, as well as to possess something of his own to command.

It is significant to note that when Penny comes to the sinkhole he expresses a similar feeling. Penny points out that his desire is for "peace." Although Jody, because of his lack of experience, does not yet understand nature in these terms—that is, as an escape from society—he displays the same type of introversion as his father. The beauty of this microcosm, as Penny puts it, is that there is nothing to interfere. In order to understand Jody, one must come to understand and appreciate the world in which he lives. Mrs. Rawlings' method in Chapter 9, then, is to place great emphasis on the details of this surrounding. The rather minute description of the sinkhole accomplishes this purpose.

Appearance and Reality.   When, in Chapter 10, Jody falls ill with a fever from eating too many brier-berries, he is confronted with the possibility for deception. He has already seen an example of this when Penny traded the feist for the new gun. He perhaps has found out from this instance that withholding a part of the whole truth is not the same as lying. Thus he goes along with his mother's assumption that he has come down with the measles. Furthermore, he is not exactly certain that the brierberries are in fact the cause of his illness, thus he does not feel fully obligated to reveal this. The extent to which his sense of morality has been developed is revealed in his feeling of guilt at not revealing that he has eaten too many brierberries. This is yet another revelation of the puritanical background represented by his father, who is the son of a preacher and is known for his honesty, having, like Abraham Lincoln, once walked a considerable distance to return an overpayment from a storekeeper. Further, this incident helps to emphasize the close male relationship between Jody and his father, since Penny goes along with Jody and does not tell Ma Baxter about the brierberries.

The Theme of Initiation.   The initiation theme is furthered in this section of the book with Jody's fishing trip and his shooting of his first deer. The fishing trip is again an incident in which the male relationship is brought out. Jody imitates his father's prowess at fishing and is able to catch a fish himself. His father is duly proud of Jody for this accomplishment, since it shows his development toward becoming adept at providing food. It may be noted that even the fishing, which is otherwise a pleasurable indulgence, also has a practical lesson in it. When Jody catches a small bass, his father makes him put it back because it is not big enough for eating and will be more useful later when it is larger.

Penny's puritanical attitude is exercised in practically everything he does. The closeness of the relationship between Jody and his father is brought out not only in their participation in fishing, but in their mutual awe at watching a flight of whooping cranes. This mutual participation in the beauties of nature brings them closer together. Significantly, they do not say anything about this and remain silent at the table when they have returned home to eat the fish. This too is a part of Jody's initiation. He learns that even though his father has much experience and lives according to the rules of practicality, still he has a sense of the wonders of nature. This point is also brought out when Penny brings in the dead albino raccoon. He is as much fascinated by this oddity of nature as Jody is. The deer hunt is another step in Jody's initiation. He is given his own gun for the first time—the old muzzle-loader his father has used. He has his own knapsack made of the skin of the albino raccoon.

This is a significant moment in Jody's life. He is now ready to take an initial step toward his maturity and to be put on his own. When he does in fact shoot the deer, though, it is an imperfect shot and his father must shoot the deer also in order to make sure it is dead. Nevertheless, the fact that Jody sat in the tree alone and shot on his own shows progress in his initiation. In addition to this he learns some of the lore of fishing and hunting. These will be necessary bits of knowledge when it comes time for him to provide for himself. So far he has not been put on his own and owns nothing of his own. He is still dependent and must learn how to take care of himself. Penny continues to emphasize that this type of knowledge is more important than schooling since it is more directly related to survival.

Grandma Hutto and Oliver.   Some critics have pointed out that the section dealing with the Huttos is the most contrived in the book. Practically every popular story of a young boy deals with the unusually enjoyable trip to Grandma's, and Grandma Hutto herself is somewhat a stock character. The grandmother of these stories usually is extraordinarily kind and jolly, allows certain liberties the parents forbid—such as allowing Jody to go swimming by himself in the St. John's river—offers unlimited food, particularly sweets, and usually lives in better circumstances than the grandchild—Penny and Jody not only enjoy a bath in the river, but sleep on a real bed with sheets. In this sense Grandma Hutto is a conventional character and does not add appreciably to the story. The only really distinctively individual thing about her is that she is not in fact Jody's grandmother. This, however, only adds to the contrivance, since Jody's actual grandmother probably would not be this way at all, judging from the severity of both Penny and Ma Baxter. There is also the conventional attitude that Jody takes: even though he greatly enjoys the freedom and abundance he experiences at Grandma Hutto's, he would prefer to be at home, since it is a more familiar world to him and one in which he is more personally involved.

Oliver Hutto, the sailor son, is also a stock character of a type to be found in many stories for boys. His returning from strange places, his wearing of earrings like a pirate, his bringing of gifts, and his tall tales of adventure are all elements of characterization long outworn in stories of this kind. He is not so much a personality in the book as a representative to Jody of the outside world, which he has not yet experienced. Thus, while Grandma Hutto and Oliver may provide interest in that they call up a stock response in the boy's life, they do not stand as individuals and do not add anything appreciably to the story as characters. This is merely a typical episode from a boy's life—one which might be expected.

Jody's Attitude Toward Girls. Two events in this section bring out Jody's attitude toward girls. The first takes place when Penny and Jody arrive at Boyles' store. The fact that Penny had previously teased Jody about being interested in Eulalie Boyles had put him on the defensive against her. Again Jody's attitude toward this girl is more or less stock; that is, it is to be expected that a boy of his age would take this attitude toward girls. Thus when Eulalie puts out her tongue at him, he is irritated and throws a potato at her. This lapse of Jody's goodness just after Mr. Boyles has complimented him on his good behavior and had rewarded him by giving him a mouth organ simply substantiates his interest in the male world with which he is becoming identified through his initiation. This, in other words, is Jody's way of showing his loyalty to the maleness which he is developing. Penny blames this action on Jody's association with the Forresters, and his reprimand of Jody by making him give back the mouth organ shows his intent to keep Jody on his good behavior. Jody had "glowed with a sense of virtue. He longed to be good and noble."

To Jody the presence of the girl is a threat to this goal which he had set up for himself. When Oliver Hutto later leaves to visit Twink Weatherby, Jody is again aware of a threat to the male world. He has already observed that his father's relationship to his mother is one of command. His mother is confined to the house and to the kitchen and not allowed to participate in the male activities or to be part of the male code. Grandma Hutto presents no threat to him since she is not in a position to threaten the male world into which Jody is being initiated. Further, the feud between Oliver and Lem over which one is to have Twink as his girl presents a situation of interference. Jody is thus inclined to see girls only as a threat to the closeness of his male relationships, and he concludes that he hates girls and never intends to have a girl of his own.

Penny's participation in the fight, and his taking sides with Oliver, is dependent only on the code. Penny

reasons that Oliver must be defended since he is out-
numbered by the Forresters. Had Oliver had the advantage, he would have defended the Forresters.
When Jody joins the fight, he does so in imitation of
his father's loyalty to this code. Another important
aspect of this relationship is the parallel with the
animalistic fight for survival in nature. Lem and Oliver fight over Twink as the bucks do over the does.
Jody sees himself as becoming a part of this struggle in
nature. At this point he resists participation in this
struggle as long as he can. When he jumps on Lem
and is knocked out, this indicates that he is not yet
ready to take his place in this struggle. Penny remarks
somewhat sadly that Jody must yet learn the ways of
women.

CHAPTERS 13–16

After spending the night at Grandma Hutto's Jody awakens
the next afternoon feeling sore from the fight. Oliver has
been badly beaten. Penny expresses his pride in Jody for his
participation in the fight. Twink Weatherby leaves town on
the river boat. Jody says goodby to Oliver and he and
Penny return home to find the hogs are missing. Penny
assumes they have been taken by the Forresters in retribu-
tion for his participation in the fight. Penny and Jody set
out toward Forrester's Island to look for the hogs. While
crossing a grapevine entanglement, Penny is bitten by a
rattlesnake. Penny shoots a doe and applies parts of its liver
and heart to the snakebite to draw out the poison. They
notice the dead doe has a fawn. Jody goes to the Forresters,
despite their falling out, to ask for help. Buck and Mill-
wheel agree to help, but Lem refuses. Jody, afraid and
alone, returns to the cabin to find Doc Wilson is there,
together with Buck and Mill-wheel. Buck agrees to stay
with the Baxters while Penny is sick. Before leaving, Mill-
wheel takes Jody to the forest to find the fawn. Jody takes

the fawn home as a pet, agreeing to give up his own milk for the fawn. That night Buck and Jody shoot two foxes that have stripped the corn field. When they return home there is a great commotion and they discover a bear in the yard. Buck shoots the bear. Jody slips out after the others have gone to sleep and brings the fawn into the cabin.

> **COMMENT: Justice.**   One of the lessons Jody learns from the fight between the Forresters and Oliver Hutto is the meaning of justice. The reader will recall that in Chapter 10 Penny and Jody had encountered a group of people called Minorcans who were hunting for gophers. Penny had told the story about how they had been promised plenty by a landowner who then abandoned them when times became bad. Penny had expressed his sorrow for these people who had been dealt with unjustly. All this had happened in the past, though, and there was not very much Penny or Jody could do about it now. But when they become involved in the Forrester-Hutto feud, they have a choice. They must decide which side they are going to be on.
>
> It must be remembered that both the Forresters and the Huttos are friends. Jody does not want to lose the friendship of either of them, particularly because he is very fond of Fodder-wing and does not wish to lose this connection. Then choice is made on the grounds that Oliver is outnumbered, and Penny remarks that it is unjust for the Forresters to outnumber him. Jody's own participation in the fight is prompted by this sense of justice, and by the moral attitude he has acquired from his father. Penny is therefore proud of Jody for taking sides in this issue and remarks that Jody is indeed a man, meaning that he has developed his own sense of moral choice. This is intensified by the fact

that both Penny and Jody undergo personal physical injury in order to uphold their sense of justice.

It may be noted also that both these incidents, the Minorcans and the fight, confirm Penny's attitude of isolation that people are most likely to interfere with each other. He does not, however, shrink from responsibility when the time comes to uphold it. Jody and Penny differ from the landowner who treated the Minorcans unjustly in that they take up their moral responsibility to their friends when it becomes necessary to do so.

Duty—Another Moral Lesson.   Jody is confronted with another moral situation in the act of revenge on the part of the Forresters. When he and Penny return home they find the hogs have been taken. When they set out to find them they discover a trap and a trail leading to the Forresters' house. The Forresters have planned to take revenge on the Baxters in this manner. Penny and Jody had both expected the Forresters to act in this manner, once again confirming Penny's view about the basic incompatibility of people and the superiority of nature. But the important aspect of Jody's moral development is not the action taken by the Forresters, but Penny's attitude toward it, which stands as a model for Jody. Penny takes the attitude that he must retrieve the hogs even at the risk of facing the ire of the Forresters. At first Jody is confused by this attitude. He cannot reconcile duty, which his mother had mentioned to him many times, with the possibility of perhaps being injured again by the Forresters. It is a conflict again between the possibility for total isolation and the force of necessity. Jody at first cannot understand why it is impossible for him to live in total isolation. But he soon comes to realize that the necessity of staying alive—of survival—makes such isolation impossible, or at least impracticable. They have to go to the Forresters and retrieve the hogs in order to have meat to live on. This is once again a great moral lesson that Jody learns: survival comes before anything else; man's peaceful natural life is limited by this necessity. Had Penny and Jody refrained from entering the fight, they would not have had their hogs stolen, but, on the other hand, they would have allowed injustice to prevail. Thus Jody learns that physical necessity and moral necessity go hand in hand. One must develop his moral sense as well as his ability to survive. Both these things are of great importance.

Ironically, just before Penny starts to cross the grapevine and is bitten by the snake he points out to Jody that one must face trouble whether he wants to or not—it is a matter of duty. Even though Penny and Jody *know* they may run into trouble from the Forresters, they are unaware of the snake hidden in the grapevine. "Trouble," as Penny puts it, may come not only from man, but also from nature when you least expect it. In either case it must be faced squarely, and, significantly, Penny does not shrink from it. Even though the Forresters are dangerous, there are even worse dangers lurking unknown and unseen. This incident helps further emphasize the life and death struggle in which the Baxters are involved. Both Penny and Jody act bravely and with calmness and endurance when danger strikes. Because Penny has prepared himself morally to meet such a crisis, he is prepared when it does strike. Then, when Jody becomes responsible for taking care of his father, who is in danger of dying, he must himself take up duty. He must go to the Forresters to seek help despite the fact they might not help him, or even do him harm.

Having learned this lesson, though, Jody proceeds to the Forresters' as his father would have done. He finds when he arrives there that the Forresters, in spite of their faults, also put their sense of duty above the feud between Lem and Oliver. Buck and Mill-Wheel agree to cooperate since a life is involved. Only Lem shrinks from this moral sense and refuses to give aid. As will be seen later, this prepares Jody to reconcile himself to the shooting of his pet fawn when this act also becomes a matter of duty and necessity. But the reader must understand that Jody does not know these things instinctively; he must learn them by example as a matter of moral development.

All this, in other words, is a part of his initiation into adulthood. Significantly, Buck not only helps to get a doctor for Penny, but stays on to take up the Baxter's farming chores while Penny is sick. This is not so much an act of benevolence as it is a function of his sense of duty. He would do this for anyone, friend or enemy, under circumstances where survival is involved. The reader will recognize this as a basic human problem of morality. Very often one is obliged to carry out such a duty even though it may be distasteful to him—sometimes even one's enemies must be helped. Lem does not take up this duty, but prefers revenge. In the end he loses and Oliver wins the girl. This is what is known as poetic justice. The shooting of the doe is yet another example of duty. This would not have been done under other circumstances, but, since Penny needed parts of the liver and heart to draw the poison from the snakebite wound in order to survive, it became a necessity.

It is significant that the fawn Jody takes as a pet is a result of this duty. Somewhat paradoxically, Jody is rewarded by an act of cruelty brought on by necessity.

Jody receives the fawn out of an act of sacrifice on the part of the doe. Out of these various examples of duty grows the idea that survival depends upon communal support. As much as Jody would like to live by himself with nature and enjoy nature to its fullest, and as much as Penny would like to live in peace without interference from others, it becomes plain that everyone is dependent upon everyone else when survival is involved: Jody and Penny had to come to the rescue of Oliver, Penny had to look for the hogs in order to assure the survival of his family, the doe had to die in order to save Penny, Buck and Mill-Wheel and Doc Wilson had to come to the aid of Penny, Jody had to face the Forresters alone, and Buck had to help with the farm work. In this is shown the impossibility of total isolation and the necessity of dependence upon others for survival. Thus in taking the fawn as a pet, Jody is not only fulfilling his desire for something to own and command, but is himself taking up a duty. He takes it upon himself to assure the survival of the fawn whose mother is dead.

Jody's Sense of Aloneness.   As a corollary to these events showing the moral importance of duty based on the necessity for communal action, there is much emphasis in this section of the book on the feeling of loneliness, especially concentrating on Jody. Not only is the fawn a companion for Jody, giving him something of his own to cling to, but Jody finds himself in the situation of loneliness when he has left the Forresters and has to return to Baxter's Island by himself. He feels very much afraid and alone in the forest by himself and imagines that he sees ferocious animals. This fear of being alone is not unnatural. He is afraid of death as well as of being unprotected. Death is something which he has to face. When he finds the fawn, at least temporarily, this fear is abated, since he feels he has something to cling to. Death becomes a reality later when Fodder-wing dies and Jody in part realizes its inevitability. Again, this prepares him for the fawn's death at the end of the book. But the fear that his father may possibly die is not yet a reality. It is a fear connected with his general feelings of closeness with his family and dependence upon them.

It is interesting to note that Mrs. Rawlings expresses this fear of the unknown in romantic terms. Natural phenomena seem to sympathize with Jody. As he is on his way home from Forrester's Island the weather turns bad and it begins to rain. This adds to the mood of the scene. Another feeling expressed in this scene is pity. Jody feels sorry for those who must of necessity be alone. He is fortunate in that he has his family and, later, his pet to keep him from being alone. Jody learns that while life may be less complicated and more peaceful without the interference of others, yet loneliness itself is undesirable and makes for fear and a feeling of helplessness.

Psychologically speaking, Jody exhibits the need practically everyone, unless he is a hermit, has for companionship, love and closeness. This need is coupled with the need for possession, which Jody expresses in his desire for the fawn as a pet. Jody's microcosm itself—Baxter's Island—represents to him a place of love and security. All around the island is the struggle for survival, one animal robbing the other for food and sustenance. Jody and Buck go and rob the bee-tree and in turn a bear comes into the yard to rob the Baxters of the honey. But they are able to ward off the intruders, and Penny eventually gets well. Thus Jody takes pride in his protection and his ability to relate himself to others. He further learns from this that since everyone is dependent on everyone else, as far as survival is concerned, there is nothing personal. Lem has not learned this lesson and stubbornly and immorally holds out from his duty.

Buck, on the other hand, serves as a substitute father and teaches Jody how to rob bee-trees and how to shoot foxes in the corn field, pointing out to him that these are serious matters—the most important part of his education. In taking in the fawn, Jody expresses his dislike for being alone and his pity for those who are. Jody finds it is much better to try to live compatibly and with compassion for others than to try to go it alone. In this sense Jody is somewhat the opposite of Huckleberry Finn, for example, who is for the most part a free spirit. Huck, at times, as does Jody, becomes very lonely, and seeks companionship, but he does not have the deep sense of insecurity exhibited by Jody, and when it comes time for him to make a moral decision, he finds the strength to stand by himself. Jody leaves home after the shooting of the fawn, but finds the warmth of home and its familiarity better than striking out on his own. Thus for Jody to know loneliness and death is a good lesson for him, since he eventually has to face this himself.

CHAPTERS 17–18

Unable to find a name for his new pet, Jody decides to go to the Forresters' and ask Fodder-wing to name him. However, his father says he must chop an entire row of sweet potatoes before noon if he is to be allowed to go. Jody does not finish the row, but his father lets him go on the condition that he bring the water from the sinkhole. The fawn follows Jody about in his work and is a playful nuisance. On the way to Forrester's Island he sees two male bears fighting over a female, an experience which very few have. When he arrives, Buck tells Jody that Fodder-wing has died suddenly and that the funeral will be held the next morning. Jody feeds Fodder-wing's pets and then sits up with the body. Penny arrives and the next morning Fodder-wing is buried. Before he and Penny leave, Buck gives Jody Fodder-wing's crippled pet red-bird named Preacher. When they arrive home they find the Forresters have returned the hogs.

COMMENT: Jody's Confrontation with Death. This is a highly important section of the book in that it represents a turning point in Jody's initiation and moral development. In the previous section he had been confronted with the *possibility* of death—his father might die as a result of the snakebite wound. But now he actually experiences this in Fodder-wing's death. His reaction to this is all-important. To a child a significant loss, such as the death of a friend, might have traumatic consequences, and it increases his need for security in the form of love and companionship. Jody is able to take this loss with some calmness because he is emotionally secure as a result of his close family ties and his ability to fall back on the mystical healing power of nature. His possession of Flag, the fawn, supplies for him such security. Also because he has learned from Fodder-wing and from his own close associations with nature the true meaning of affection, he does not feel bitter or cynical about Fodder-wing's death. Jody's first reaction as he sits with the lifeless body of Fodder-wing is one of fear—he sees the formless ferocious animal lurking in the corner of the room. Then he thinks of death as a silence, and is despondent about this. But when he goes to the sinkhole after returning home, he finds in this symbol of his security and the strength of his isolation that Fodder-wing's spirit persists in nature. When he sees at the sinkhole a raccoon with its two young, whom she feeds and reprimands by spanking, he feels the presence of Fodder-wing and his closeness to nature. He has a private spiritual feeling which he is unable to convey in words even to his father. The reactions of his parents to this death are also revealing of Jody's character. Once again Penny looks upon his participation in this event as a duty and remarks that even though he had to associate with the Forresters, who had acted immorally and taken revenge on him, people are the same at the core regardless of how they may act in their relationships with one another.

In his prayer at the graveside when Fodder-wing is buried, Penny reveals that he looks upon the death of Fodder-wing as his release from misery. He regards the death from this point of view as benevolent. He has strength in this matter since he has lost several children himself. Ma Baxter takes a more cynical attitude, remarking that she wished it had been Lem, since he is so black-hearted. Her attitude is that toughness—developing a hard attitude toward life—is the best way to deal with it. Thus there are three attitudes expressed toward this death, or three types of solace. Jody finds release in nature and the companionship of the fawn; Penny sees the death as a blessed relief and as a sign of the communality of human emotions; and Ma Baxter chooses to take a hard attitude, buttressing herself against such catastrophes by avoiding emotional involvement. The Forresters, who are unprepared in any of these ways, take the death very hard. Jody's feelings are conveyed in the fact that Fodder-wing had given the fawn its name. The lame red-bird which Buck gives Jody upon his departure from the Forresters is symbolic of the continuing presence of Fodder-wing.

The "Mystic Company" of Men.   Another aspect of Jody's initiation and his moral development is embodied in his encounter with the male bears who are fighting over a female bear. This is a lone, private experience which he has, and one which he is privileged with, since not very many people would ordinarily come upon such a scene. In a spiritual sense Jody identifies with the bears, which themselves are chief inhabiters of the natural world, being the most powerful and cunning. This warring experience of the bears is one which Jody is approaching as an adult and one which is fully understood only by the males. Jody remarks that this is an experience which he will possibly be able to convey to generations younger than himself in future times, just as the adults about him do in the present. The fact that this is a mysterious, private experience ties in with his feeling about Fodder-wing and his relationship to nature. Jody's awareness of the presence of death following this experience of seeing the bears relates the two together. Symbolically the bears stand for fear and death. It is Jody's chief fear regarding Flag that the bears might kill him for food. All of this looks forward to the later section in the book when Slewfoot, the most powerful bear of all, is killed. By this time Jody has reached a point in his maturity when his childhood fears are abated.

Foreshadowing. Previously it was mentioned that foreshadowing is one of Mrs. Rawlings' primary structural devices in this novel. In this particular section of the book foreshadowing is an important element in that the reader is prepared for the section to follow in which there is almost the opposite condition to that existing in the present section. The present section shows the Baxters in a state of plenty: there are long rows of sweet potatoes, plenty of corn is growing, the peas are making good, and Buck had shot the bear, giving them extra meat. In addition they have the hogs and the honey gotten from the bee-tree. Jody himself is in a state of happiness and security since he has at last gotten a pet. Further, the bad relationship between the Baxters and the Forresters has been at least temporarily patched up. This abundance of food and of happiness and security makes even more desolate the catastrophe that falls when the rains come and the crops are ruined. Also Jody's encounter with death and the loss of Fodder-wing looks forward to the time when he must give up his pet fawn.

CHAPTERS 19–25

The Baxters enjoy their plenty and the crops are growing well. But bad weather comes, and persists for eight days. The Baxters try to save the crops as best they can, but most of them are destroyed by the heavy downpour. The water has spread everywhere and many wild creatures have drowned. Penny and Jody notice that some animals have died of black tongue, a plague. Slewfoot gets into the yard and kills a hog, so they decide to kill the rest of the hogs and prepare them for the winter's food supply. Flag gets into the potatoes and Ma Baxter becomes angry. A pack of wolves comes into the yard at night. Penny and Jody go out to shoot them, but they run away. Penny goes to the Forresters' and they decide to set poison for the wolves, despite Penny's objections. The Forresters go with Penny and Jody on a hunt. They kill two deer and two bears and take ten bear cubs captive. On the way home Penny kills a buck. The Forresters agree to take the bear cubs to Jacksonville and trade them for supplies. The Baxters go to Volusia to buy supplies and Christmas presents for each other and visit Grandma Hutto.

COMMENT: The Other Side of Nature.   Whereas in most of the rest of this novel nature has been presented both as beautiful and peaceful (with the exception of the maraudings of Slewfoot, the bear) and as serene and mystical, this lengthy section deals with the other side of nature: the storm, its aftermath and the plague that follows. As has already been pointed out, the snake hidden in the bushes served as a sort of forewarning of what might come later. In a certain sense, Fodder-wing's death also was a forewarning in that he was most closely associated with the serene in nature. Now, during the September storm season, we see the fury of nature, exhibited in the wind and rain and the floods that cover the surrounding territory. Survival becomes of utmost importance to beast and to man. Man's smallness—and even the smallness of animals—is brought out. Against the forces of nature, man is sometimes defenseless. All of man's most highly developed sense of survival is put into play.

Importantly, Mrs. Rawlings concentrates on the survival power of the Baxters. They are prepared for the storm, and so are able to survive it without severe damage. This seems to parallel their moral preparation—they have prepared themselves morally also to withstand any onslaught from outside. Furthermore, they are undaunted in their efforts to restore their lost crops and to prevent further marauding by bears and wolves. Their endurance is put to the test, and, instead of giving in, or making excuses, they stoically bounce back to make a recovery.

Although Mrs. Rawlings does show some of the destructive side of the storm—animals die, the plague strikes, the wolves ravage the barnyards—she rather assumes an optimistic view of man's place in this onslaught. It is, once again, because of preparation, because the Baxters have carried out their duty, that they can survive. Not only do they survive, but they profit by this onslaught. The bears and deer they kill and capture, to great advantage to themselves, are a product of this storm since they are driven to high ground and are made easier to capture. The security of the home prevails over the storm brought upon it from outside. It is the pioneering spirit of endurance that Mrs. Rawlings most concentrates upon. Her conclusion about this bad side of nature seems to be that even though bad times may come, there is a good side: for every black cloud there is a silver lining. Further, man can survive even the worse times if he is prepared to do so and has built up his capacity for endurance.

Legend. In the beginning discussion of this book we noted that one of the characteristics of the traditional type of society is that its "literature" is made up not so much of the printed word (the Baxters never read anything, except on rare occasions when Jody might take out his spelling book, or when Penny reads the note on Doc Wilson's door) but of events that either (1) are immediately observed, or are in the process of taking place, or (2) have taken place in the past and survive in stories passed on by word of mouth. We also observed that these stories are usually closely related to morality, and that they present a model for the younger generation. Much of this section of the book is taken up with these two types of legends. Before proceeding to examine these, a further distinction might be made. There is also the difference in legends about events that seem to have some survival in the present and those that are actual fact. The legend of the Spaniards falls into this first category. Frequently Jody thinks he sees these Spaniards, but the members of the older generation discount these stories since, even though the Spaniards did in fact pass across the Florida hammock country at one time, this actual occurrence does not exist presently in anyone's memory. These legends, however, show one's relationship to the past, and their similarity to the actions of the present insure the continuity of the past.

Significantly, the hunting stories told by Penny and the other adults also show this continuity and thus insure continuity. That is to say that what is taking place in the present, primarily adventure and heroics connected with hunting, is essentially the same as what has taken place in the past. The conventional, traditional line has not been broken and there is assurance that things will go on as they have in the past. This is a preoccupation of traditional societies and a method of setting examples and models for generations to follow. Thus the major preoccupation of the Baxters, for example, as regards Jody is to make sure his experience remains the same as theirs.

In this particular section of the book there are several such stories illustrating the way in which Jody is trained or initiated. This carries with it the idea, as Grandma Hutto had once expressed it, that learning from experience is more important than learning from books. Jody's formal training is thought of by the Baxters but not emphasized. The type of language used by the Baxters, Ma Baxter's display of ignorance of syntax when she corrects Jody, and the list of supplies, misspelled and poorly expressed, show a minimal amount of formal knowledge. Further, as has been shown, Jody's moral training and his training in the ways of survival are held to be most important. He learns morality primarily from experience—from moral actions actually undergone. This may occur both in hunting when courage and fortitude come into play and in human relationships. For example, when Lem attacks Penny thinking Penny has lied to him when he said he would not pursue a buck on the way home from the hunting trip, Jody expects Penny to fight back. But Penny explains his reluctance to do so on the grounds that he need not make the same display of uncontrolled anger as did Lem. This stands as an example of goodness to Jody.

Another aspect of legend as displayed in this section of the book is that it usually springs from the unusual. Mrs. Rawlings spends a great deal of time on the storm and its aftermath and the plague as an example of the unusual. This is a legend in the making in that it is an unusual occurrence. This is the first time even in the lifetime of the adults that such a storm has taken place. They have never had any experience with a plague. Thus this is something that will be remembered long after, primarily because it sets an example for action. At first no one knows what to do and all their past experience must be brought into play. The exact moral reaction is put into play in the question as to whether to set poison for the marauding bands of wolves. Penny objects to this on the grounds that wild creatures should not be treated this way even when they pose a threat to survival. The Forresters do not hesitate to do this. Ma Baxter's view that Penny's goodness sometimes outstrips practicality is another possible attitude toward morality. That is that adjustment, or modification, in one's moral position must be made where survival is concerned.

Eventually Penny's position prevails when some of the Forresters' dogs are victimized by the poison. The unusual character of this legend, then, not only provides a tale that will possibly be handed down through generations but has the effect of producing a new principle of moral choice. It is significant that Jody is almost casually caught up in this unusual set of events. When he shoots his first bear it goes almost unnoticed, and he hardly thinks about it himself. This is because he is an integral part of the events taking place—an almost equal member of the "mystic company" of men. It is not a question of training or initiation since, under the unusual circumstances, he is as much a part of these events as the adults, who themselves operate in these events without precedent. The ordinary run-of-the-mill deer hunt, for example, which might be re-enacted many times, is a training ground based on precedent, but the shooting of several deer, Jody's shooting the bear and the taking of ten live bear cubs, is a new experience in which Jody is an equal participant.

The War of Nature. Mrs. Rawlings was aware, although she does not emphasize this, of the theories of Charles Darwin (1809–1882) that greatly influenced many writers in her time to deal with the struggle of man versus nature and man versus society. In this section of the book there is a strong suggestion of what Darwin called the war of nature, or survival of the fittest. The smaller animals are destroyed by the larger ones. The most powerful and crafty, the wolves and bears, prevail over other less fit animals. Predatory animals, like the wolves, take advantage of helpless animals, like the Baxter's heifer which is trapped in the corral, and prey upon it because it is defenseless. The Baxters and the Forresters themselves take advantage of the deer and bear trapped by the high waters, unable to defend themselves in the usual manner. Nature itself supplies these animals with food and they ordinarily keep to themselves when this provision is plentiful, but when the food supply is diminished by the flood and the plague they must turn to other sources and the wolves, who usually stay away, come into the Baxter's yard. Darwin concluded from his theory that man himself is a superior creature who was best able to survive many centuries of this war and was not created separately from the other animals but emerged as a higher form of animal as a result of his necessity to survive. A great deal of the training, and experience, which Jody goes through is directed toward his survival in this war. Significantly, he is not only protected, but becomes a protector when he takes in the fawn. His constant fear is that the fawn will become a victim in this war of nature and he gains confidence and security as a protector.

It may be noted that the primary basis for conflict in this story is the war of nature of which the people are a part. Their houses, Baxter's and Forrester's Islands, are frequently referred to as fortresses in this war. The conflict is not so much man versus society as it is man versus nature. Whenever there is social war, for example in the feud between Lem and Oliver, this closely parallels the war of nature. The two bears Jody sees fighting closely parallel Lem and Oliver fighting over Twink Weatherby, and Lem has an almost animalistic reaction to this conflict.

Delaying Action.   One of the structural purposes of this section of the book is to delay the climax of the main story line. Up to the point when the storm struck, two main story lines had been developed: Jody's relationship to the fawn and the feud between Lem and Oliver, incidentally involving the Baxters. The device of building up to the resolution of such conflicts and then holding off the resolution is not unusual in this type of novel. Throughout this section, most of the action is diversionary—that is, it has little to do with the actual furtherance of the major story line as it has been set up in terms of suspense. Also it may be noted that since one of Mrs. Rawlings' primary structural principles is to base the action on the rotation of the seasons during a single year, this period of the year must be taken into account. The climactic action thus comes at the end of the year.

CHAPTERS 26–27

Christmas is not far away and the Baxters make preparations to attend the celebration at Volusia to be held on Christmas Eve. Four days before Christmas, Buck comes by to say that Slewfoot has killed the Forresters' hog. Penny puts a trap in the yard, but Slewfoot comes in and kills the newborn calf. Determined to kill Slewfoot, Penny and Jody set out to hunt him. Julia trees Slewfoot and Penny wounds him. Penny and Jody spend the night at the house of the widow Nellie Ginright. The following morning they set out in an old canoe and Julia jumps Slewfoot in a thicket. At high noon they catch up with him and Penny shoots him. The Forresters come along on their horses and they take the bear back to Baxter's island in pieces. Then they proceed to Volusia where the Christmas celebration is taking place. They discover that Grandma Hutto's house is afire after the Forresters learn Oliver and Twink have returned on the river boat and that they are married. Even though the Forresters have started the fire, in order to avoid bloodshed, Grandma Hutto tells Oliver she had left a lamp near an open window. Grandma Hutto leaves with Oliver and Twink to live in Boston. The Baxters return home.

COMMENT: Slewfoot.   This section of the book is taken up primarily with the killing of Old Slewfoot, the bear. The reader will recognize this as one of the basic stories in American literature and legend, probably having been passed down from Indian ritualistic and initiatory legend. Probably the best known such story is William Faulkner's *The Bear* (1935, 1942). There are many parallels in Mrs. Rawlings' story to the basic traditional legend. The bear itself is unusual, weighing some five hundred pounds and having, as is usual, a mutilated foot as a result of once having been caught in a bear trap. This not only makes the bear unusual but shows its extraordinary ability to elude traps which other lesser bears might be caught in. In addition to these distinguishing characteristics, the bear is regarded as somewhat human, and at the same time a sort of god. This bear, alone among the many bears in the area, is given a name as though he were human. Also he is given to human emotions. When Slewfoot comes into the Forresters' corral and kills their hog, he does this in a fit of anger, a fight, rather than for food. When the bear kills the Baxters' calf, he leaves the carcass not far from Baxter's Island. It is out of "meanness" that he kills, not out of necessity for survival.

Also, as has been pointed out, Slewfoot is an embodiment of fear and menace, like the gods and devils of ancient, pre-civilized times. Francis Lee Utley, the critic, writing about Faulkner's bear, Old Ben, remarks that he "has cosmic dimensions; he is the God of the Wilderness." The fact that Slewfoot has roamed the woods for many years and has killed often out of what the people regard as meanness, and that he is widely known as a legendary being, sets him apart from the other wild creatures as the embodiment of evil and as the epitome of evil forces in nature. The human quality of Old Slewfoot is also brought out when he is finally shot. Although the hunt itself had been intense, difficult and treacherous, the bear seemed to give up at the end and just sat down. "It seemed so easy now that it was over," Mrs. Rawlings remarks. Old Slewfoot, in other words, simply gives up. He is old and his time has come. The point is not so much that Penny and Jody have been able to outwit the bear, but that, like a human, the bear simply dies when his time comes to do so.

The intensity of the hunt itself becomes ritualistic. It is unusual in that it is more difficult and more treacherous than most hunts. The quarry itself is more dangerous and there is more at stake. When the hunt begins Penny has little regard for teaching or initiating Jody —he would just as soon have left him behind. The Christmas function is put aside in the seriousness of the moment. Jody even allows Flag to go astray in the woods at the risk of great danger. Jody and Penny agree that "Huntin's a man's business." Penny himself is described as being in a "grim mood," and vows "hit's me or him." All of Penny's energy, all his hunting experience and all his wisdom and craftiness come into play. This is not a pursuit for food—it is not a matter of survival, but a matter of morality: "This was hate and revenge and there was no happiness in it." For the first time Jody finds Penny "cold and implacable."

All this seems to indicate that what Penny is going after is something larger than himself or the bear. He intends to destroy what the bear stands for: possession of the natural world. This is a final showdown as to who will be boss in the war for survival. The victory itself cannot be directly attributed to Penny, but to man himself and to man's sense of morality and fair play. It is significant that Old Slewfoot, like Faulkner's Old Ben, does not follow the rules, the code. Old Slewfoot does not show up at the carcass of the slain calf as Penny expects him to do on the basis that other bears would do this. He does not follow the trail as is expected. Furthermore, Slewfoot kills not for food but for revenge.

It has been established at this point that Penny, who studiously and honestly follows the code, would not kill except for food. But Slewfoot, like the Forresters, who are also renegades who do not follow the code, would. This gives Penny justification for killing the bear, although, as Penny says after he has shot Slewfoot, he has great respect for him because of his prowess and great capacity for endurance. All these stories about bears who are powerful and godlike, but who are finally killed by men, include this respect, and they all show the bear violating the code, thus giving man a justification for the kill. This seems to point out that man is superior after all since he is capable of developing a rational code of honor—a morality based on fair play. The animal is not and must finally be destroyed. This is why the pursuit of this singular bear is always considered of the highest seriousness having an epic quality. It is a final, or ultimate, test of man's morality. Ritualistically man wins out over the bear because of man's capacity for reason, which allows him both to build a code and to live by it.

It is noteworthy that this final moral battle takes place in the woods, in isolation, far from society. It is like a religious ritual between man and God and is exclusive of man's relationship with himself. This is ritualistically undertaken under the most trying conditions. It is winter and ice is everywhere. The cold and the necessity for keeping on the track of Slewfoot almost without letting up put the hunters to an ultimate test. This then becomes the primary legend, which Jody is allowed to share in and which he will pass on to following generations. In a sense this killing of Slewfoot is a beginning and an end for Jody. It signals the end of his period of initiation and the beginning of the time when he will have to make decisions for himself.

This decision soon confronts him when it becomes necessary for Ma Baxter to shoot Flag.

The Forresters.   As might be expected, the Forresters are engaged in frivolity at a time when seriousness is most called for. Instead of pursuing Slewfoot after he has killed their hog, they get drunk in celebration of Christmas and are on their way to Fort Gates for further frivolity at a time when Penny is being most serious and taking up the pursuit. Penny himself remarks later than anyone with a serious enough intent could have caught up with the bear. But, as usual, the Forresters shun their moral duty. It is only after the kill when the thing has been accomplished and finished that the Baxters celebrate. Then they sing songs and attend the celebration. Once again duty comes before pleasure with the Baxters. The Forresters continue their frivolity when Buck puts on the bearskin and scares the people at the Christmas party in the church at Volusia. He does this without regard for the safety of others or for his own safety. Penny has to stop him to keep him from being shot. Mrs. Rawlings seems to be saying that the serious accomplishments are to be made by those who have serious moral intent.

As a final act of immorality the Forresters set fire to Grandma Hutto's house. This act is doubly dastardly because Grandma Hutto, who is innocent of the quarrel between Lem and Oliver over Twink Weatherby, is made to suffer. However, her goodness is shown when she lies to Oliver, telling him she had left a lamp near an open window thus causing the fire. It is perhaps difficult to believe that Oliver would have believed this so easily knowing the Forresters were given to such acts. But it also shows his innate belief in Grandma Hutto and his unwillingness to believe she would lie to him. This is accepted, even by Penny, on the grounds that bloodshed between Oliver and the Forresters would have been worse. There is thus a sharp contrast between Penny, who takes up his moral duty even at great risk and difficulty, and the Forresters who continue in frivolity and end in a completely immoral act.

Delaying Action.　　Another example of Mrs. Rawlings' use of delaying action as a structural device occurs when Penny and Jody spend the night at Nellie Ginright's house. The story of the bear hunt itself constitutes a tale within a tale. That is, it has a separate suspense and climax of its own. Will Penny catch up with the bear? If and when he does, what will happen? Will the bear get away again? The answers to these climactic questions are held off in the interlude while Penny and Jody go into the house, find that the widow is not there, make supper and spend the night. When she does come the next morning, the discussion between Nellie, whom Penny had courted at one time, and Penny further holds off the action. The reader is held, as it were, in suspension while these events take place. This must, from the writer's point of view, come naturally, and Mrs. Rawlings accounts for this delay on the grounds that Slewfoot had crossed the creek and the dogs would not follow. It was thus necessary for Penny and Jody to take a circuitous route and follow the bear on the creek. If this delaying action had merely been a contrivance it would not have been believable.

CHAPTERS 28–33

Returning to the safety of Baxter's Island, the Baxters lead a leisurely life. Flag begins to grow, and Jody takes up Penny's chores while he is ill with rheumatism. Flag begins to show signs of wildness and Jody has to tie him up. However, this is not a solution and Flag gets into more and more mischief. Penny tells Jody to take the yearling to the woods and shoot him, but Jody is unable to do this. He goes with Flag to the Forresters' to ask them to keep Flag, but the Forrester boys are gone and their parents refuse him. When he returns home Ma Baxter shoots Flag, wounding him. Jody shoots him again, killing him. He then leaves home with plans to go to Boston and join Oliver there. He takes the dugout from Nellie Ginright's and sets out, but hunger and exhaustion overcome him. He is picked up by the mailboat and taken to Volusia. He decides to return home. Penny takes him back and Jody agrees to stay on at the farm to take up the work his father had begun.

COMMENT: The Moral Resolution. As has been seen throughout the discussion of *The Yearling*, the principal preoccupation of the major characters concerned is morality. There is a concerted effort to act according to principles of goodness and nobility in any given situation. This principle is founded upon the basis of survival, and survival itself is foremost above anything else. Coupled with this is the necessity for facing the requirements of survival. One of these requirements is manhood, or maturity, and Jody's basic training, through his initiation, is led in this direction. Thus it is natural that the resolution of the basic moral problem should be in terms of Jody's ability to face a dire moral decision as a man. He has been fully prepared for this inevitability—that is, the fact that he must one day give up the innocence of his childhood and face the world as a man.

This crisis comes when Jody must give up Flag, a symbol of his childhood and immaturity and a parallel in nature. In this section of the book Mrs. Rawlings

leads up to the moral resolution by pitting the wildness
of the untamed yearling against the necessity of survival, represented by the crops. The moral resolution
is also led into by a close parallel between the two
"yearlings": Jody and Flag. All of these things lead up
to the final moral decision Jody must make when the
yearling is killed. He at first blames this on the betrayal of his father. He comes to this conclusion, that
his father has betrayed him, on the basis that Penny
had told him he would save the yearling at any price.
It is only later that Jody realizes the real meaning of
necessity. When the Baxters first return from the
Christmas celebration at Volusia, Jody is overcome
with a sense of security and well-being. His loneliness
is taken up by his companionship with Flag. Further,
he feels a strong sense of responsibility and fulfillment
as a result of the contributions to the farm work he
makes while Penny is ill with rheumatism. Jody has
been trained well. He is obedient and helpful, but he
does not yet realize the meaning of this obedience and
of the moral development he has passed through.
When a wolf comes into the yard and plays with the
dogs at night, Ma Baxter comments on the loneliness
of the wolf, but Jody does not relate himself to this
loneliness. To him it is still remote. Neither does Jody
immediately realize the relationship between himself
and the yearling.

When the yearling begins to show his lack of tameness,
Jody seeks to make up for this by overseeing his pet.
But the yearling is a wild creature which cannot easily
be tamed. Jody picks up the dried peas after Flag has
spilled them and replants the tobacco after Flag has
trampled in the bed, but this does not constitute disci-
pline. The first lesson that Jody learns from this is that
wrongdoing, or wildness, cannot be made up for by

someone else, rather it must be prevented altogether. Merely undoing a wrong is not enough. Once the damage has been done, it is sometimes too late to make up for it. Even though the tobacco and peas and corn can be replanted once or twice, time will soon run out and it will be too late. Jody then tries preventive measures. He and Ma Baxter build a fence, but the fence is not high enough and the yearling finds a way through. This is not only costly in time and effort, but it is ineffectual. The only possible way to prevent disaster is to train the animal properly.

The point is that Jody, as a yearling, can be trained. He can be made to be obedient and good, because he has the faculty of reason. The animal, on the other hand, goes by instinct, and this instinct cannot be removed. Lawful behavior, therefore, depends upon rational behavior based on good. As hard as Jody tries to make Flag good, he cannot reason with him and therefore cannot control his behavior. Jody must be punished in order to understand this himself. Thus when Flag gets into the corn field and eats the shoots for the second time, Ma Baxter realizes he must be shot. Jody's immediate reaction that he hates his parents is in fact an expression of general hatred for the cruelty of life. It would be much better if he and Flag could both remain free, but the necessities of living demand that they both be tamed.

Jody's withdrawal from nature is, then, a part of his maturity. Up to this point he has had an innocent, spiritual relationship with nature, as Fodder-wing did, but at the point when Flag is killed he must give up part of this relationship in favor of necessity. At the end of the book, Mrs. Rawlings' image of the dead Flag and of the lost innocence of Jody fading into the forest indicates the final passage of this purely non-practical attitude of Jody's—it is the end of innocence.

Stoicism. The dictionary defines a stoic as "one who bears suffering impassively; one who keeps his feelings rigidly controlled." This is in essence the attitude finally adopted by Jody after the pattern of his father. After Jody has returned from his attempt at escape, his father points out to him that he must simply take things as they come. Penny himself has set an example for Jody by stoically enduring his rheumatism, by continuing his struggle against great odds in the hammock country despite his small stature and his lack of help, and finally by enduring the suffering of his rupture without complaint.

How does Jody finally come to the decision that he must remain on the farm and endure not only the loss of the yearling, and his childhood, but whatever the future may bring for him in this desolate area? We have already seen that Jody made up for his loneliness and lack of security by attaching himself to the pet yearling. But, after he loses this pet, he must attempt other means. He first turns to the Forresters, but finds them gone. The Huttos are another possibility, but it is foolishness to think that he can get to Boston, and his attempt to do so by paddling up the river fails because he is overcome by hunger and exhaustion. It is again hunger that forces him to this decision. He finds that no matter how hard he tries, this is something he cannot overcome simply by willing to do so. It is, in other words, necessity that forces him to take things as they are. He has done everything it is possible to do to avoid this, but it is something which at last stares him in the face. Penny offers the possibility that he, like Oliver, could go to sea as an adventurer, but Jody finds that he is attached to the familiarity and security of the farm. He arrives, then, at this stoical position since there is no better possibility.

This feeling is further intensified by his feeling of loneliness in the forest and in the dugout after he has left home. Even nature feels alien to him and hostile. When he attempts to build a flutter-mill in the creek where he once did, this also is something alien and without meaning to him anymore. He comes to realize that the harsh demands the world would put on him would not be worth the effort. He has no will to change anything, to try to make the world different. Thus his stoical position is in fact the easiest way out, and he is not a rebel. He finds that the demands of survival make it necessary to accept things as they are without complaint. The land will provide him with food and his parents with a sense of security. They are at least somebody to be wanted by. His conclusion about the world outside Baxter's Island is that he is not wanted by this world. It is a hard lesson that Jody learns in terms of the story, but the difficulty of the lesson makes it easier finally for him to accept.

In this experience Mrs. Rawlings sees a leading argument for the necessity of law and obedience. If the yearling had been allowed to run free, everyone would have suffered. It remained for Jody to know hunger first-hand in order for him at last to realize the necessity for law and order. The simplicity of these people, the Baxters, who make no attempt to change things points up at least one aspect of human life—the need to provide for one's livelihood. Thus Penny's conclusion that "life goes back on you," and Jody's decision that one must "take it for his share and go on," shows the pioneer spirit of stoicism, which is the opposite of rebellion.

Loneliness.   One of the major decisions put to Jody in this section of the book is the possibility of going it alone. This is in fact the decision he makes when he leaves Baxter's Island in his attempt to go to Boston. This is a possibility which is perhaps put to everyone. We saw in the beginning that Penny moved his family to Baxter's Island in order to get as far away from society and its ills as possible. But he found he was nevertheless dependent, at least to an extent, on the outside world. He had to trade at Volusia, he needed the Forresters on occasion, as when Buck came to work on the farm, he needed the doctor and he needed the help of his wife and son. Nobody could exist altogether by himself, and isolation, as has been shown, is a destructive thing in itself. Jody felt a real need for companionship and thus took the pet fawn.

In leaving home Jody is put to an actual test to see if he can survive on his own. He puts the final shot into Flag at the sinkhole, which at one time had been the place of his security and of delight in being alone in his own imaginary world. But now this is spoiled by the sight of his dead pet. They will no longer play together on the side of the sinkhole. Jody finds that he needs more than this. But he does not fare well by himself. He is not able to provide for himself. Neither is he able to convince anyone to agree with him. Ma and Pa Forrester side with Ma Baxter and agree that the yearling has to be shot. The men on the mailboat on the way to Volusia feed him, but they are indifferent to his loneliness and remark that no one would have much sympathy for him. Thus loneliness drives Jody to seek the best of the two possible worlds— going it alone or returning to the security of his home.

His final conclusion is that it is best not to try to face the world alone. Even the wolf that comes into the yard at night wants companionship and must suffer for the lack of it. Everyone must have the feeling that he is wanted by someone else. Jody's real feeling of manhood finally comes, then, when he feels he is needed by someone else and that there is a definite place in life for him. With his father ill, it now becomes his responsibility to take care of the stock and the crops. Everyone is lonely in the sense that life goes back on him, as Penny put it, but this particular loneliness can be overcome if one is needed—if there is some responsibility for him to assume. This is what constitutes Jody's maturity, his passage from childhood and innocence to becoming a "yearling" and then to becoming a man.

CHARACTER ANALYSES

JODY: The only surviving child of the Baxters, he is sensitive and lives close to nature, which he loves. In the largest sense he is a model child. He is obedient and works hard without grumbling or questioning the reasoning of his superiors. Jody is dealt with in this book as he grows into maturity and we see him going through the cycle of seasons in a single year. His moral perception is developed as he takes part in the activities of the world of men into which he is about to pass. His sensitivity is brought out in his reactions to the killing of animals for food. He understands the necessity of this, but is repulsed by the sight of the dead carcasses and by the idea that slaughter is necessary to existence. Many of the attributes of Jody's character may be said to be common to boys of his age, despite the fact that Jody lives in virtual isolation and within a relatively small range of experience. What perhaps makes Jody different is the intensity of his love for nature and the ability he has to give himself wholly to his pet.

PENNY BAXTER: Perhaps the most complex character in the book because he is the only one to whom motives are attributed. The fact that he has come to live in the remote hammock country is attributed to some past hurts he has had. He has been in the war and hints at other wounds to his psyche. The difficulty of the life led by the Baxters seems to indicate that it would be better for them to move somewhere else. But Penny has a native distrust for people and does not wish to live among them. Penny himself, as Jody does gradually, loves the natural surrounding in which he lives and derives much pleasure from his ability to provide for himself under trying conditions. He takes an almost martyred attitude toward his existence in that he forces these hardships upon himself. Living the type of life he does gives Penny the chance to be a hero in his own context. But Penny's basic attitude is one of stoicism. He believes that one must accept the world as it is and make the best of it. Whatever happiness he has grows out of his sense of accomplishment under trying conditions. He is a good father and a good husband, and, above all, serves as a good model for Jody as he is growing up.

MA BAXTER: Although Ma Baxter (also known by her first name as Ora or Ory) is sometimes shown as an individual personality, she is intended primarily as the prototype of the frontier wife. She reflects the now largely outdated concept that the wife's place is in the home. Expectations of her do not extend beyond her household responsibilities, though these are definite and are left entirely up to her to perform. Unlike Penny, Ma Baxter is intolerant of any kind of action that is not altogether serious. This is one of the reasons why she prevents Jody from having a pet and disapproves of it when he does. She has a typically feminine attitude toward other women and takes this out especially on Grandma Hutto, whom she considers frivolous and foolhardy. That Ma is not altogether without feeling is shown when she breaks into tears upon being given a gift of alpaca by Penny. She simply buries her emotions in favor of the necessities at hand. Ma in part proves her point when she shoots Flag. She can do this impassively not only because it is a necessity, but because she knows it will be best for Jody to build up an immunity to disappointment.

FODDER-WING: This lame son of the Forresters who has gotten his name from his attempt to jump from a barn using fodder as wings symbolizes devotion to nature without responsibility. He is a foil to Jody in the sense that Jody also is sensitive and loves nature, but, being normal and fully rational, also must be responsible. Jody learns from him the value of ownership and of extending one's love to a creature. When Fodder-wing dies this is Jody's first encounter with death. Fodder-wing's death gives Jody a premonition of a more severe loss to come.

BUCK FORRESTER: Buck stands as an example of the basic goodness of man despite his faults. Although Buck drinks and carouses with the other Forresters and spends much of his time in frivolity, he is a good friend when he is needed. He is pleasant and of an even temper. Because of his basic goodness, Jody learns much about becoming a man as a result of his relationship with Buck.

LEM FORRESTER: The only really bad character in the book, Lem constantly shows himself to be self-centered, hot-tempered and vindictive. He is lawless and without conscience. He stands as a model to Jody of what would happen if people were set free to do as they wish.

GRANDMA HUTTO: Probably the most stock character in the book, Grandma Hutto is pixyish and coquettish, thus bringing down the disfavor of some. Her general attitude toward life is one of pleasantness and permissiveness. Her age and experience give her an advantage, but it is her capacity to take a bright, optimistic attitude toward things and her ability to bounce back from whatever setback befalls her that makes her admirable. Probably one of her major characteristics is that she refuses to fall in with the general social expectation of the place of women. In addition to this, she is a typical storybook grandmother dispensing food in abundance, sweets and good cheer.

OLIVER HUTTO: Oliver serves mostly as a symbol to Jody of the outside, adventuresome world. He is the typical sea-going adventurer with a ring in his ear bringing back exotic gifts from far-away places. He stands as a model for Jody of the possibility of escape from the farm.

CRITICAL COMMENTARY

Since it has not been widely accepted by serious critics of American literature, the only available criticism of this book is contained in the reviews that immediately followed its publication in 1938. The reviews were almost universally good. Typical of the comments was that of Frances Woodward in *The Atlantic Monthly* of June, 1938. In praising Mrs. Rawlings for the clarity and simplicity of her style she added that "She has captured a child's time sense, in which everything lasts forever and the change of season takes him always unawares." William Soskin, writing in *Books*, April, 1938, pointed out that "Jody Baxter is the most charming boy in the entire national gallery." He goes on to compare Jody to St. Francis, who was also a lover of nature and of wild creatures. The *Time* reviewer pointed out that although the book was written for younger readers, it could also be enjoyed by adults as well. Nearly all the reviews were especially praising of Mrs. Rawlings' style which allows the reader to feel the presence of Jody and his world, and her ability to capture with accuracy and fidelity the natural surroundings in which Jody lives. The very lack of psychological probing and of explanation probably has kept the book from receiving more critical attention than it has. Modern critics are more apt to be preoccupied with works given to Freudian analysis, intricate structural design, prolific symbolism or sophisticated study of individual or social behavior. The fact that the book was chosen as the Pulitzer Prize Novel for 1938 seems to be its highest praise.

ESSAY QUESTIONS AND ANSWERS

1. What is the chief moral lesson that Jody learns?

ANSWER: Primarily that as one grows into manhood, he must give up certain things he has cherished as a child. The demands of living make it necessary to turn away from what Jody at the last of the book refers to as "play-dollies." In order to become a man, one must take on responsibilities that have to do with the necessities of living. At the beginning Jody finds it is possible for him to indulge in dream-world pastimes, such as building flutter-mills and romping with his pet fawn. But he must soon turn to more serious matters, such as learning to hunt, to rob bee-hives and to plant and care for crops. There are certain duties that must be performed and it takes both knowledge and courage to carry them out. At the same time these duties are being carried out, one must retain a sense of justice and right for those who deserve right. Thus Jody learns that it is not good to kill simply for the sake of killing, but only when it is necessary. Finally, he has to give up the thing he loves the most—his pet Flag. But in so doing he learns the meaning of necessity and the requirements of a manly attitude toward loss of his childhood with its innocence. His idyllic childhood must give way to responsibility at last. The chief lesson Jody learns, then, is to be a man. This entails obedience, attention to duty and the realization that survival itself comes before anything else.

2. What is the significance of the relationship between the Forresters and the Baxters?

ANSWER: The Forresters and the Baxters represent two different levels of society in the hammock country. While the Baxters are always sober and moral, the Forresters are given to frivolity and amoral attitudes. The

Baxters make their living honestly from the land while the Forresters bootleg and trade for a living. The stature of the Forresters and their black, hairy appearance makes them more animalistic than the Baxters. Penny and Jody are both small and must make a more difficult struggle for existence. This contrast allows the author to point out characteristics of both by virtue of the differences involved. Thus the contrast itself is used as a structural device to bring out the characters of members of both of the families. Although the Baxters and Forresters have frequent fallings out, they will help each other in times of need. The relationship between the two families also shows the need they have for each other. Neither of them could exist without the help of the other. In showing these two families, Mrs. Rawlings shows two types of inhabitants of the Florida hammock country.

3. What is the function of nature in the book?

ANSWER: Nature is primarily a provider. Part of the tension in the lives of the Baxters grows out of the fact that they must live from nature while at the same time they have a great deal of love for it and a mystical relationship with it. This is brought out in Jody's attitude toward the killing of game for food. Thus they must see nature in two lights: both as provider and as something beautiful to be enjoyed almost to the point of worship. This is why Mrs. Rawlings spends a great deal of effort in describing in minute detail the birds, trees, animals, wild and tame, and the countryside in general. The people live very close to nature and therefore are very much affected by it. The simplicity of the lives of those who live this close to nature is reflected in nature itself. Also reflected in nature is the struggle for existence. The people observe the animals as they struggle to survive and carry out their mating and familial functions. Just as with the animals, the people are subjected to both sides of nature, the good and the bad. The attitudes of people are reflected in these good and bad sides of nature. They are sometimes friendly and sometimes hostile. It is man's place to subvert nature to his own uses and the education Jody goes through is primarily concerned with his study of nature and its ways. Since this has most to do with survival it is more important than knowledge he may gain from books and he spends most of his time in this study. Jody also learns that nature, as well as sometimes being hostile and alien, can be a solace and a place of inspiration. Jody is attracted to nature and its representatives, like Flag, because it is wild and free, but he must learn to reject that which cannot be tamed.

4. What is the major attitude toward life expressed by the Baxters?

ANSWER: Mrs. Rawlings seems mostly to have been impressed by the fact that the Florida hammock country people withstood a difficult life always tottering on the point of starvation without complaint or rebellion. Their attitude of stoicism and undying optimism seems foremost. Even after the devastating storm followed by a plague Penny remarks that it is not much of a world to live in but the only one we have. The general attitude is to make the best of what there is. The Baxters take great pleasure in the smallest gifts. They derive most of their fun from telling stories, talking to the townspeople in Volusia and making visits to Grandma's. Theirs is not an exciting life, but it has its drama in the hunts, the fights and the small, everyday conflicts with nature. The main point is that they do not give up whatever the odds. Whenever they are down they get up again and try again. Just to be alive and to have some food to eat is enough for them to thrive on. The desires of these people are not great. There is not much they want beyond that which is necessary. The Baxters criticize the Forresters for having guns they do not actually need or use. It is considered sinful for there to be anything surplus or merely for the sake of luxury. This is a pioneer attitude, based on utilitarianism, which still persists in American thought. All this is backed up by a stoic rejection of pain or suffering. To some these people may seem strangely anachronistic since the average character in the modern novel is rebellious and unwilling to accept things as they are. Huckleberry Finn is rebellious, for example, in that he refuses to accept things as he finds them. He constantly tries to change his condition and the conditions of society. This quality of stoic acceptance is perhaps what attracted Mrs. Rawlings most. It is certainly a part of the American character and of the American moral point of view.

5. What are the chief characteristics of Mrs. Rawlings' style?

ANSWER: Since Mrs. Rawlings worked as a reporter she learned much about objectivity in writing. In addition to being objective, that is, keeping her emotions and feelings out of the story, she is detailed and accurate. A concerted effort is made to tell the story on the basis of accurate detail about the countryside, the living habits and the people themselves. Most of what the author has put into the book is in the nature of first hand reportage rather than imagination. Only the plot itself is the result of a great deal of imagination. The accuracy of detail is obvious in the dialects used by the people. Further objectivity is witnessed in the fact that she does not explain motives or probe psychologically into the minds of the characters. The book gives the impression, as a result of the style, of a letter or a report written on a visit to some strange land as though no one else had ever been there.

NOTES

NOTES

NOTES

NOTES

NOTES

NOTES

NOTES

MONARCH® *NOTES* AND STUDY GUIDES

ARE AVAILABLE AT RETAIL STORES EVERYWHERE

In the event your local bookseller
cannot provide you with other
Monarch titles you want –

ORDER ON THE FORM BELOW:

TITLE #	AUTHOR & TITLE (exactly as shown on title listing)	PRICE
	PLUS ADDITIONAL $1.00 PER BOOK FOR POSTAGE	
	GRAND TOTAL	$

MONARCH® PRESS, a Simon & Schuster Division of Gulf & Western Corporation
Mail Service Department, 1230 Avenue of the Americas, New York, N.Y. 10020

I enclose $ .... to cover retail price, local sales tax, plus mailing
and handling.

Name _____
(Please print)

Address _____

City _____ State _____ Zip _____

Please send check or money order. We cannot be responsible for cash.